Spiritual Source of Guidance

Pastors
Preach but Have
No Power

Written by Pastor ***Anita Riley***

AuthorHouse™
1663 Liberty Drive
Bloomington, IN 47403
www.authorhouse.com
Phone: 833-262-8899

Because of the dynamic nature of the Internet, any web addresses or links contained in this book may have changed
since publication and may no longer be valid. The views expressed in this work are solely those of the author and do
not necessarily reflect the views of the publisher, and the publisher hereby disclaims any responsibility for them.

Any people depicted in stock imagery provided by Getty Images are models,
and such images are being used for illustrative purposes only.
Certain stock imagery © Getty Images.

This book is printed on acid-free paper.

ISBN: 979-8-8230-1261-4 (sc)
979-8-8230-1260-7 (e)

Print information available on the last page.

Published by AuthorHouse 07/31/2023

authorHOUSE®

To my church family, First Harvest Faith Christian Center. Also, to Min. Felder, Min. Sloan, Deacon Fairly, Evan. Anthony, Sis. Johnson, my very dear friend Ralph Watkins, my children Ernest and Elonte Riley, and my only grandchild, Miss Yaniya Riley, the little lady who runs the house, just to name a few.

I'd like to thank you all for keeping me in your prayers and pushing me. Thank you for seeing the greatness in me when I didn't see it in myself.

Contents

Introduction..v

The Power of God's Word...1

The Power of the Pastor 6

God's Word and the Pastor 12

The Fall of the Pastor..16

The Comeback of God's Pastors 25

Introduction

The Bible holds supreme authority over all creation and this world. Who is the King of Creation? God himself, the Supreme Being. Scripture is God's revelation in our history. It can open up doors to our spirits that we have never imagined. It has the power to bring any dead situation to life, and we will see that situation live again. Psalm 118:17 tells us that I shall not die but live, and declare the works of the Lord. Can I get an amen to that?

As I started writing this book, God showed me so many things. Pastors, bishops, apostles, evangelists, and so on do so many things that do not line up with the Word of God, yet we still see them in the pulpit and wonder why there is no power coming from the pulpit. We as people of God need to take a look at ourselves and get this right. We need the Holy Spirit to flow freely in God's temples. We think God is pleased with us when we get up before His people and speak a feel-good sermon. But what about the anointing flowing in the temple to get people delivered? We are so wrapped up in the money or the prestige that it brings us; we forget the reason we are out front: to bring *glory* to *God*. Not self. Think about it. Are you glorifying self or God?

To all my fellow pastors and Christians partners, this book is not written to bring anyone harm or to judge anyone. I am not writing this to talk about anyone in particular; this is just a book that God put on my heart. So as you read this, read with an open mind.

The Power of God's Word

The Power of God's Word

God's Word is living, and it does exactly what God says it can do. When I look at the Word of God, it tells me that power is in His Word, which we can read and get results. We will get the right outcome every time if we are lined up with the Word of God.

"For the word of God is quick, and powerful, and sharper than any two edged sword, piercing even to the dividing asunder of soul and spirit, and of the joints and marrow, and is a discerner of the thoughts and intents of the heart" (Hebrews 4:12). If we take a deeper look at that scripture, we find the power of God's Word. It is living, it is active, and it cuts through all the infirmities that come with everyday life. It tells me that it speaks to the heart and mind and it tells them to line up with the Word of God. It tells me that God knows my thoughts and the intentions of my heart. We as a people may not know another person's motives, but the Word tells us that God knows and that He will see to it that His Christian people will not be left in the dark. Now *that's* power.

"So shall my word be that goeth forth out of my mouth: it shall not return unto me void, but it shall accomplish that which I please, and it shall prosper in the thing whereto I sent it" (Isaiah 55:11). This means God is not all talk. When He talks, His words accomplish His intended purpose. The Word of God has power, and it never fails or fades away from that intended purpose. That's a powerful thing to think about because people will have the best intentions. But their endeavors may not produce the results they were looking for.

That is not the case with God's intentions. Not ever.

I cite many scriptures because I need you to see just how powerful God's Word is. It is nothing to be reckoned with. It is powerful and must not be ignored. It is a force within itself.

"In the beginning was the Word, and the Word was with God, and the Word was God. The same was in the beginning with God. All things were made by him; and without him was not any thing made that was made" (John 1:1–3). This tells me the role of God as Creator is established in verse 3. The universe is not the product of mindless matter but of an intelligent Creator who is more powerful than the human mind can imagine. Jesus is said to be identical to God, which makes them one. So the scripture makes the point that nothing created was created apart from Jesus. This proves that Jesus was with God because He is the Word; He carried the Word here on Earth. This shows us that there is one thing that has always existed: God Himself, the Son, and the Holy Spirit.

We are still talking about the power of God's Word. "For the preaching of the cross is to them that perish foolishness; but unto us which are saved it is the power of God" (1 Corinthians 1:18).

You have to realize the Word of God may seem foolish and disagreeable to carnal people's minds. They cannot get it because they are too busy looking for something they can see or touch. The Word of God will never get them delivered, because people try to understand the power of God through their own minds and rationalities. They will never be delivered this way. You need to be a born-again Christian to understand God's Word and how it works. Without God's spirit living and moving upon you, it won't happen; you will keep twiddling your thumbs and pondering over God's powerful words.

"It is the spirit that quickeneth; the flesh profiteth nothing: the words that I speak unto you, they are spirit, and they are life" (John 6:63). It is the spirit of God that quickens him or her or begins to breathe into that person; then he or she becomes a living soul, for the body without the spirit is dead. It is lifeless; the spirit of God enters a person and brings life. The Word of God is the spirit that gives life and is the savior of life, but it comes not only in words or in ministry but through the Holy Ghost and the power of divine grace.

"Now the parable is this: The seed is the word of God" (Luke 8:11). As we look at this scripture, we find that Jesus used parables so that the believers could understand His message.

It was also a defense so Satan would not know what Jesus was talking about. The power of God's Word is still working today all around us—just look and see.

"In the beginning God created the heavens and the earth. The earth was without form and void, and darkness was over the face of the deep. And the spirit of God was hovering over the face of the water. And God said *let there be light*" (Genesis 1:1–3, emphasis added).

Look at the power of God's Words. Everything that happened in Genesis 1 was done because of the power of those Words. God spoke and it happened. Read Genesis 1. Those of you who have never picked up God's Word are in for an awesome surprise. God created everything by His words. He spoke it and it happened.

God's words still have power. Every time I look at a verse it talks about the power of God's Word. We need to get this in our spirits, there is much power in the Word of God, whether we want to believe it or not.

"But the word of God grew and multiplied" (Acts 12:24). God's Word tells me that it is powerful because the Word of God increased and multiplied. This tells me the Word of God was spread all over the world by godly men and women, and it didn't stop reaching the people that it was intended for. God's designed His Word to heal the land.

"Every word of God is pure: he is a shield unto them that put their trust in him" (Proverbs 30:5). Every Word of God is pure, which means we can depend on Him. His Word will do what God set out for it to do. We as believers should know that if we trust God, He will provide and protect us from all evil. God's Word does not lie. We should live, eat, and sleep in His Word.

"Heaven and earth shall pass away, but my words shall not pass away" (Matthew 24:35). This tells me that the Word of God has an assurance, that His Word has vitality and endurance with the mightiest works of this world. No matter what comes against God's Word, it will never fail. It will stand its ground without any help from humankind.

"He sent his word, and healed them, and delivered them from their destructions" (Psalm 107:20). Man is not healed by medicine alone but by the powerful Word of God. Man has been restored from being put into the grave. God's Word will do it and has done it in the past. People will be delivered from their own destruction by the power of God's Word.

The heavens proclaim the glory of God. The skies display his craftsmanship. Day after day they continue to speak; night after night they make him known. They speak without a sound or word; their voice is never heard. Yet their message has gone throughout the earth and their words to the entire world. God has made a home in the heavens for the sun. (Psalm 19:1–4 NLT)

We are surrounded by displays of God's craftsmanship. The heavens give evidence of His power, love, and care. The universe did not just happen by chance; God Himself created it when He spoke His Word in Genesis 1. God is all powerful, and He is just. His Word will, can, and is justified. He needs no help.

"But Jesus told him, 'No! The Scriptures say, People do not live by bread alone, but by every word that comes from the mouth of God'" (Matthew 4:4 NLT). Remember when Jesus was led by the spirit into the wilderness to be tempted by the devil? The devil tempted Jesus three times, but Jesus used his God-given power against the tempter. We as believers have the same power, but we don't use the Word of God the way Jesus did in the wilderness. The Word of God is inspiring, uplifting, energizing, and encouraging. It is life, hope, peace, and love. With all those things that God's Word is, it can be nothing but grace and mercy. His grace and mercy are the divine influences for us to be able to endure the trials of life and resist temptation. They inspire us and impart strength into us.

Grace is unconditional love toward people who may not deserve it. No matter what we do, God always shows His total love. He is always just.

Mercy is showing compassion or forgiveness when it is within one's power to punish or harm. God gives all of this to us in His Word. If we just take the time to meditate on it, we will see all things in His Word come to pass. The Word of God is life!

My question to you is, have you tried or will you try His Word?

The Power of the

Pastor

The Power of the Pastor

The pastor should have spiritual gifts to operate in the house of God and will carry a plethora of responsibilities. The Greek word for pastor is *poimen*, which means shepherd or overseer. Do you know how many responsibilities those titles carry? In the Bible, shepherds had many responsibilities solely in the care of their sheep. The shepherd kept a lookout for predators and protected his flock from any attackers. They also had to care for the sick sheep, and they had to ensure that the flock stayed together. If one were to wander off the shepherd was responsible for guiding them back to the herd. It is said that the sheep can recall the voice of their shepherd.

"My sheep hear my voice, and I know them, and they follow me" (John 10:27). Pastors are called shepherds because they watch over God's people, His sheep. Pastors who are chosen are gifted to watch and care for the spiritual well-being of a local body of God's people. In Matthew 22:14, Jesus tells us "many are called, but few are chosen." When you are called, God needs you to handle a specific matter. When you are chosen, you have a responsibility to carry out for God what will not fade away. Preachers are God's servants to God's people on Earth. Some of them may be the closest things we will ever see to God while we are here. God has given them specific orders to carry out for the will of His people. The pastor's goal is to reveal God's glory by and through the Holy Spirit.

"So Christ himself gave the apostles, the prophets, the evangelists, the pastors and teachers, to equip his people for works of service, so that the body of Christ may be built up" (Ephesians 4:11–12). Pastors should have the gift of teaching. They should be able to teach scriptures so plainly that a little child could understand.

"The teaching of your word gives light, so even the simple can understand" (Psalm 119:130 NLT).

"He must have a strong belief in the trustworthy message he was taught; then he will be able to encourage others with wholesome teaching and show those who oppose it where they are wrong" (Titus 1:9). Pastors must believe what they speak and must have the knowledge, wisdom, and power to break the Word down into simple statements—not changing the Word, just making it understandable for everyone. Another virtue that a pastor must have is the Holy Spirit. Without the Holy Spirit, you will never be able to convert others. You must be able to cause change through the power of God's Word.

"Now unto him that is able to do exceeding abundantly above all that we ask or think, according to the power that worketh in us" (Ephesians 3:20). We can ask the Holy Spirit to fill every area in our lives, because as people of the cloth, we need God's guidance every second of our lives. When we guide people, we need to be led in the right direction as well so that we will not get off track. If we get off track, we may lead God's people astray, the same way a shepherd becoming distracted may lose a few sheep.

We have a major decision to make when it comes to answering the call of God. As people of the cloth—as bishop, apostle, pastor, or prophet—we need to hear the voice of our Creator so we can rightly divide the Word to minister to God's people.

"Study to shew thyself approved unto God, a workman that needeth not to be ashamed, rightly dividing the word of truth" (2 Timothy 2:15). Having the mind of Christ, we must be Christian. We must also be doers of the Word and have faith and *believe* in the Word. We have the power living inside us, so we can and should guide people in the right direction. Guiding them in the right direction will help them become saved, sanctified, and filled with the Holy Ghost.

> 1Out of the stump of David's family will grow a shoot yes a new Branch bearing fruit from the old root. 2And the Spirit of the Lord will rest on him the Spirit of wisdom and understanding, the spirit of counsel and might, the Spirit of knowledge and the fear of the Lord. 3He will delight in obeying the Lord. He will not judge by appearance nor make a decision based on

hearsay. 4He will give justice to the poor and make fair decisions for the exploited. The earth will shake at the force of his word, and one breath from his mouth will destroy the wicked. 5He will wear righteousness like a belt and truth like an undergarment. (Isaiah 11:1–5 NLT).

If we call ourselves bishop, apostle, pastor, reverend, prophet, or evangelist, we should walk in the same spirit, as the scriptures above tells us. It tells us how Jesus will be and still is today. We should walk in that same power, in that same spirit, and in that same holy grace. "But you will receive power when the Holy Spirit comes upon you. And you will be my witnesses, telling people about me everywhere—in Jerusalem, throughout Judea, in Samaria, and to the ends of the earth" (Acts 1:8 NLT).

Jesus has instructed us (His pastors) to tell the world about Him and bring people unto God. That is the power Jesus has bestowed upon pastors.

> I am the true grapevine, and my Father is the gardener. He cuts off every branch of mine that doesn't produce fruit, and he prunes the branches that do bear fruit so they will produce even more. You have already been pruned and purified by the message I have given you. Remain in me, and I will remain in you. For a branch cannot produce fruit if it is severed from the vine, and you cannot be fruitful unless you remain in me. (John 15:1–4)

We have the power to bear fruit. We have been given that power through Jesus Christ, God's one and only Son. You must work with the power you have been given by the Father. God has cleansed his pastors, bishops, and apostles from all dishonesty, jealously, malice, adultery, and lying lips. With all these things being pruned from us we have the power within us to bear good fruit and bring people to God. As long as we stay connected to the master's hand, we have the power to do all things through Him who strengthens us (see Philippians 4:13).

"A soft answer turneth away wrath: but grievous words stir up anger" (Proverbs 15:1 King James Version). In other words, we should know how to speak to our congregation without stirring up anger.

"The tongue of the wise useth knowledge aright: but the mouth of fools poureth out foolishness" (Proverbs 15:2 KJV). Ask yourself, do I have the tongue of a wise person or the tongue of the foolish? The tongue of the foolish stirs wrath.

"The eyes of the LORD ARE IN EVERY PLACE, BEHOLDING THE EVIL AND THE GOOD" (PROVERBS 15:3 KJV). WHAT DOES GOD SEE IN YOU? LET IT BE THE GOOD. WE PEOPLE OF THE CLOTH HAVE AN IMAGE TO UPHOLD. THAT IS WHERE THE POWER OF GOD MOVES INTO PLAY. ARE YOU WILLING TO LET GOD TAKE OVER YOUR LIFE SO THAT HIS WORK MAY BE DONE ON EARTH?

"A WHOLESOME TONGUE IS A TREE OF LIFE: BUT PERVERSENESS THEREIN IS A BREACH IN THE SPIRIT" (PROVERBS 15:4 KJV). AS PASTORS, WE SHOULD USE GENTLE WORDS AND NOT CRUSH PEOPLE'S SPIRITS. WE SHOULD BE LOVING, KIND, HUMBLE, MEEK, GENTLE, GIVING, AND CARING. THESE ATTRIBUTES GIVE US THE POWER TO BRING PEOPLE TO CHRIST. IF YOU HAVE THESE TRAITS INSTILLED IN YOU, IT WILL ENSURE THAT YOU ARE BRINGING PEOPLE TO CHRIST INSTEAD OF PUSHING THEM AWAY. SOMETIMES WE HAVE TO STOP TALKING AND ALLOW THE PEOPLE TO BE DRAWN BY THE SPIRIT. SOMETIMES

"Anyone who believes in me may come and drink! For the Scriptures declare, 'Rivers of living water will flow from his heart'" (John 7:38 NLT). When Jesus said living water, He was talking about the Spirit that lives in Him. We as people of the cloth should have that same spirit and that same power Jesus had when He walked this Earth. When we speak, people should listen because with the power that Jesus carried with Him, people stopped what they were doing and took notice. That is the same thing that should happen when we speak. People should stop and take notice because they identify the power, which is the same power Jesus carried with Him.

And he gave some, apostles; and some, prophets; and some, evangelists; and some, pastors and teachers; for the perfecting of the saints, for the work of the ministry, for the edifying of the body of Christ: till we all come in the unity of the faith, and of the knowledge of the Son of God, unto a perfect man, unto the measure of the stature of the fulness of Christ: that we henceforth be no more children, tossed to and fro, and carried about with every wind of doctrine, by the sleight of men, and cunning craftiness, whereby they lie in wait to deceive; but speaking the truth in love, may grow up into him in all things, which is the head, even Christ: from whom the whole body fitly joined together and compacted by that which every joint supplieth, according to the effectual working in the measure of every part, maketh increase of the body unto the edifying of itself in love. (Ephesians 4:11–16)

When we can bring all our gifts together, we are united in Christ, and love is the way to offer God's throne to God's people. Please remember, no gift is better than aanother. Everyone is placed here with certain gifts and missions in Christ. We have to unite our gifts, because power is in the ministry when we are united, not in just one person.

God's Word and the Pastor

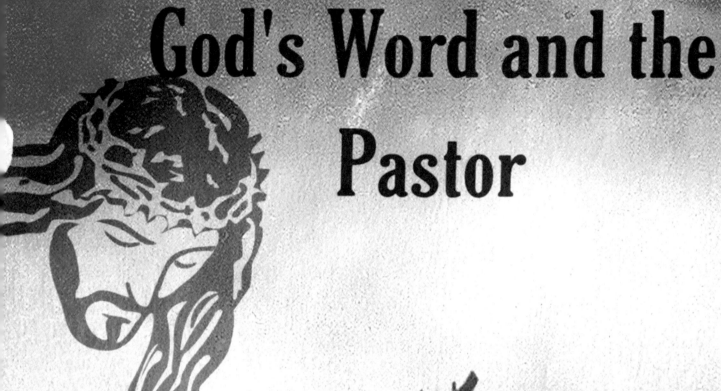

God's Word and the Pastor

"**F**aith comes by hearing, and hearing by the word of God" (Romans 10:17). As pastors, even we need to sit still and listen to the Word of God. This will help keep us humble before God.

"For I am not ashamed of the gospel of Christ: for it is the power of God unto salvation to every one that believeth; to the Jew first, and also to the Greek" (Romans 1:16 KJV). The only way we can help get God's people saved is through the power of God. We also must not being ashamed to share God's Word at any moment's notice. We as people of the cloth must speak of God's Word in season and out. His Word is the same yesterday, today, and forever. That is one thing I love about God's Word: it will never change. Amen. His Word is enough to hold you up when everything around you is falling apart; God is there to see you through. Hold on, the pastor's help is on the way! Don't give up! Stay in the race.

"That if thou shalt confess with thy mouth the Lord Jesus, and shalt believe in thine heart that God hath raised him from the dead, thou shalt be saved" (Romans 10:9).

God has given us the power to bring people to the altar for salvation by the Words He has put in our spirits. We should be able to bring God's people to His glory through our testimony. Pastors, don't be afraid to tell your story. It is not for you but for someone who is going through what you went through. There is no way to know who your testimony might minister to.

There is nothing greater than your own testimony, your own life experiences. Your testimony may help lead someone to Christ. God has given us a power within to bring light on the outside for someone else. We can only get people to the altar by our past and present situation. Why be afraid to tell your story?

No one has been saved all their life. I know I wasn't. I was a wreck undone. No one but God could have pulled me out of the mess I had made of my life, but look at what God has done! I would have never known that we could have a café, a church, houses, land, and faithful church members. (I was saying how God has blessed our church to have so many things by being obedient to his word)That is truly a blessing from God's power, glory, grace, and mercy.

"And be not conformed to this world: but be ye transformed by the renewing of your mind, that ye may prove what is that good, and acceptable, and perfect, will of God" (Romans 12:2). We need to transform our minds daily so they can line up with the mind of Christ. This is a story we have to tell ourselves day in and day out because the enemy comes daily to steal, kill, and destroy our thought processes. As God's children, we need to transform our minds and keep it in our hearts that God is working on our behalf. Our entire being should be wrapped up in the will of God, which is where our strength comes from—not from ourselves but Jesus Christ.

"I beseech you therefore, brethren, by the mercies of God, that ye present your bodies a living sacrifice, holy, acceptable unto God, which is your reasonable service" (Romans 12:1).

As I sit here thinking about all the times I did not honor God, myself, or my body, I was just in the world doing anything and everything I thought I was bad enough to do. But one day I heard a bishop say in Maryland,near Washington DC "Your body is holy." From that moment on I took notice and got into God's Word. I learned so many things I thought were right were actually wrong. Now I am a new creature in Christ Jesus. Now I can, will, and do present my body as a living sacrifice, holy and acceptable unto God. When we know better, we do better. (Well, at least some of us do.)

Pastors, what are you doing with your bodies? Are they holy?

To be holy is to be free of sin. I know some of you will say well Jesus died for our sins. Yes, he did, but nowhere in the Bible does he tell us to keep sinning just because we are forgiven or because he died for us. We have the power to live free of sin. I have met people who think that there aren't any real pastors in the world because a lot of pastors are doing the same things that the world is doing. What do you think? Are there any real pastors out there still holding the Word of God down?

"Howbeit when he, the Spirit of truth, is come, he will guide you into all truth: for he shall not speak of himself; but whatsoever he shall hear, that shall he speak: and he will shew you things to come" (John 16:13). When Jesus was speaking here, He told His disciples that whatever He speaks, it shall come directly from His Father in heaven. He was telling them that He can only speak what God tells Him to speak, nothing more, nothing less.

The spirit will help guide us so we can discern right from wrong, and it will give us insight into the future. We have this type of power if we just allow God to guide us in the right direction. True pastors have the gift of perspicacity. This allows us to discern whether a person's spirit is connected with the Holy Spirit. We have the power, the same power Jesus carried with Him because He knows his Father. If we know the Father in heaven, then we have the right to use God's power and speak to God's people with authority.

"Verily, verily, I say unto you, except a corn of wheat fall into the ground and die, it abideth alone: but if it die, it bringeth forth much fruit" (John 12:24). We as pastors need to die of self and the world in order to do God's work. The Holy Spirit is ready and willing to operate in us if we let Him have control. If we die of self, we can bear much fruit. That's the power we can have if we are just willing to remove self.

"But Jesus beheld them, and said unto them, With men this is impossible; but with God all things are possible" (Matthew 19:26). The things that may be impossible for people pose no problem for God because as Jesus said, with God all things are possible.

"1He that loveth not knoweth not God; for God is love" (1John 4:8). When we look at John 3:16, we find that God so loved us that he gave His only son. Would you have given up your only child for a world that loves sin? God loves with the agape love, unconditional love, unselfish love. No matter what you do, what you say, or where you go, God is going to love you.

That's the power we as pastors should have in our hearts as we follow Christ. We should have compassion and mercy on God's people no matter what they have done. We need to have the same love and the power that Jesus had and used when He walked the Earth. If you have faith and believe that you can and turn from your sins you can do and have the same power that Jesus carried here on earth. That's what I believe.

"And we have known and believed the love that God hath to us. God is love; and he that dwelleth in love dwelleth in God, and God in him" (1 John 4:16). We have all been redeemed by God's love when He sent His only Son to the tree to take up our sins and destroy the work of Satan and his angels. We are free if we have the faith and if we believe and receive the power of Jesus. We have the power in God's Word. When we have the Holy Spirit dwelling in us, we can conquer things that we could not conquer in our own power, such as demons, witches, and warlocks. That's the power that we will gain.

"No weapon that is formed against thee shall prosper; and every tongue that shall rise against thee in judgment thou shalt condemn. This is the heritage of the servants of the LORD, and their righteousness is of me, saith the LORD" (Isaiah 54:17–18). *Hallelujah!* Let me get my shout on!

That's the power in God's Word that gives us authority to crush anything that does not line up with the Word. My question to the pastors, prophets, evangelist, bishops, apostles, and ministers is, do you have the power God has given you, or do you merely proclaim to have it?

The Fall of the Pastor

Sometimes people of the cloth become arrogant and forget the reason God put us in positions of power. When things do not happen as we plan, we as people walking under Jesus's authority occasionally fall because of our own needs, not the needs of the people. We want the biggest churches, finest cars, biggest houses or the most members. Some people will do anything to get these things with no regard for the people they may hurt for their methods of gain. It is possible to tear down what you and God have built by becoming egotistical and losing focus.

Pastors fall every day because of greed. Instead of trying to do God's work, they lie, steal, cheat, and make false accusations to get what they want. Are we real men and women of God? I would really like to know that answer.

I have seen so much backstabbing in the body of Christ that it causes me to go into deep prayer. Pastors will slander other pastors just to try to get ahead. I pray for our clergymen and clergywomen to get their hearts and minds right with God. I am not saying I do everything right; who does? I'm striving to make heaven my home. We are all human, but as people of the cloth, we need to get our acts together before we can preach to the people of God. Now and again it is the preachers who keep people from coming to Christ, just because of their ways.

"He that answereth a matter before he heareth it, it is folly and shame unto him" (Proverbs 18:13). This is a major scripture when it comes to pastors. We may speak too quickly and cause a negative impression. We may speak before we hear the voice of the Lord, which can lead people astray, even if we have the best intentions.

"He that keepeth his mouth keepeth his life: but he that openeth wide his lips shall have destruction" (Proverbs 13:3).

"Time to rend, and a time to sew; a time to keep silence, and a time to speak" (Ecclesiastes 3:7). There is a time to keep quiet and a time to make your voice heard. If we learn to keep silent and speak at the right time, there will be no destruction, but a lot of people cannot do that because they want things to happen in their time, not God's. In certain situations, we may get the things we thought we wanted just to find out it really wasn't what we wanted at all. We must humble ourselves and wait on the Lord, so when God decides to give you something, it will be because He did it. We make an absolute mess by trying to do things of our own accord.

"When pride cometh, then cometh shame: but with the lowly is wisdom" (Proverbs 11:2). Pride brings a person to contempt and destruction. We as pastors should not allow our pride to get in the way. It can cause us to fall, and we won't know how to get back up. That is displeasing to God.

"He that is void of wisdom despiseth his neighbor: but a man of understanding holdeth his peace" (Proverbs 11:12). As pastors, I think we need a lot of work in this area. We are just like the ungodly people of the world. We say whatever we want to say whenever we want to say it. This is just like being a hypocrite, for it is ungodly to speak if the Lord is not behind it.

"The tongue can bring death or life; those who love to talk will reap the consequences" (Proverbs 18:21 NLT). Death and life are in the power of the tongue. We speak too much negativity into people's lives. We should be helping give people life, hope, joy, and freedom. How can a person be free when the pastors are binding them?

"A soft answer turneth away wrath: but grievous words stir up anger" (Proverbs 15:1). A genuine pastor should have the power to control our words, but some of us do not. Some of us don't know how to seek God before we speak. We want people to see that we are better than the next pastor, or more knowledgeable. This walk with Christ is supposed to be about saving people's souls. Many pastors love to impress others rather than humbling ourselves and learning to help each other with our weaknesses. Jesus encouraged and built up His people. Are we not supposed to be an example of Christ?

Jesus never tried to exalt himself over anyone. He was always humble. On the other hand, I have seen pastors play against each other, trying to see who can preach the best, who has the most members, the biggest church, or most expensive car. All these things mean nothing if you are not saving people's souls and changing lives. Jesus was not concerned about the house, car, church, members, or who preached the best. He lived to save souls and forgive all transgressions. God gave me my gift and he gave you your gift no one pastor preach like another pastor all our gifts are deferent and come from God.

"Whoso keepeth his mouth and his tongue keepeth his soul from troubles" (Proverbs 21:23). Pastors, guard what you say! It is ungodly to think of yourself as above anyone else. We are to be as Jesus was when He walked the earth, but we have become too much like the world. That is why we do not have the power to cast out demons or to heal the sick.

"But be ye doers of the word, and not hearers only, deceiving your own selves" (James 1:22). When we as preachers hear the Word, we need to conform to the Word just as everyone else does. We want to preach the Word but not live it. We want to live the Word in front of our church family but live another way in the comforts of our homes. So that leads me to ask, are we really *for* the ways of the Bible? Everyone we preach to is supposed to be doers of the Word, right? So how is it that we as pastors are not living accordingly? *That* is the reason pastors are preaching but have no power. In order for us to have what Jesus had, we need to be doers and live this Word and have faith and believe that we have the power to do as Jesus did… Most of us will never see the power of Jesus working in us because we are of little faith.

Some pastors get in the pulpit and fake the anointing, which is why the Holy Spirit cannot and will not move in some of these sanctuaries. When you pretend to praise the Lord for show, title, or money, we will never produce the anointing. It is time to *wake up, pastors*! Did God put you in His pulpit, or did you put yourself there? Has God really chosen you as a pastor?

"If any man among you seem to be religious, and bridleth not his tongue, but deceiveth his own heart, this man's religion is vain" (James 1:26). If you claim to be religious but do not control your tongue, you are fooling yourself, and your religion is worthless. Why do we claim to be religious but our lives do not show it? We want people to follow us when we cannot even follow Jesus. That is why some have no power. We need to take a good look at our own lives before we try to tell someone else how to follow Christ. Some of us need to sit down and pray and seek God's wisdom, knowledge, understanding, and power.

As we seek God, He will open the right doors for us, not the same ones we open for ourselves. If we allow God to humble us and lead and guide us, we will be ready for our followers. It may take some time for God to do some work in us, but as long as we stay on His path, we as pastors will make it. Stay focused on God's Word.

"Wherefore lay apart all filthiness and superfluity of naughtiness, and receive with meekness the engrafted word, which is able to save your souls" (James 1:21). We as preachers have no power because we do unrighteous things and expect God to bless our homes, children, and ministry. It does not work that way! As followers of Christ, the things we do wrong will be accounted for.

I know someone is going to say God has forgiven us for our sins. Yes, that is true, but you will have a heavy penalty to pay at the end, or it may happen immediately. You do not have to exalt yourself; God will do that when He is ready. You do not have to worry about people praising you. Nor should you worry about people trying to bring you down when you don't do something they want you to do. Don't let people exalt you, let God do that. When God exalts, you will never have to look over your shoulders in fear of people. Do not let a scandal be in your mist.

"Out of the same mouth proceedeth blessing and cursing. My brethren, these things ought not so to be. Doth a fountain send forth at the same place sweet water and bitter?" (James 3:10–11). As pastors, we should not behave as the unsaved do, but some of us do just that. The next time you get ready to do something, ask God first. Just as the fountain cannot produce two flavors of water simultaneously, we cannot speak blessings and curses simultaneously. People do this and then wonder why they are ill and diseased. They wonder why they get into the pulpit and the Holy Spirit does not manifest itself.

> Not every one that saith unto me, Lord, Lord, shall enter into the kingdom of heaven; but he that doeth the will of my Father which is in heaven. Many will say to me in that day, Lord, Lord, have we not prophesied in thy name? and in thy name have cast out devils? and in thy name done many wonderful works? And then will I profess unto them, I never knew you: depart from me, ye that work iniquity. (Matthew 7:21–23)

The reason you can cast out demons in Jesus's name is because God cannot go back on His Word. If you call on the name of Jesus, it shall come to pass. God did not say you had to be saved in order to use His name. Even if a sinner calls upon the name of Jesus, God must perform His Word. Just like if a sinner pay his tithes God has to honor his word.

"A good man out of the good treasure of his heart bringeth forth that which is good; and an evil man out of the evil treasure of his heart bringeth forth that which is evil: for of the abundance of the heart his mouth speaketh" (Luke 6:45). My question to you is, what is in your heart? Do you really have the answer? Does your heart harbor evil or good? Let God do a good work in you. We need to submit our whole heart, mind, body, and soul to God so we can stand righteous on that great day of judgment. Hallelujah.

"Jesus answered and said unto them, Ye do err, not knowing the scriptures, nor the power of God" (Matthew 22:29). I have seen so many pastors not using their Bible when they preach. How is the congregation to know what's in God's Word and what is not? The pastors will have no power because they don't know God's Word. On the other hand, they *may* know the Bible but withhold it from their members in order to keep them in bondage. That particular pastor has no power at all and does not want the congregation to have any power either. There will be no power to fight off demonic spirits. The pastor here is living a lie! We need to wake up and really become as Jesus was. He cast out demons, healed the sick and diseased, fed the five thousand, and raised Lazarus from the dead. What a mighty God we serve!

We all make regular mistakes, but being a dishonest pastor makes us no good to stand before a congregation. We need to look in the mirror and ask ourselves, "Would God be pleased with me?" Most of us can truly say no, God would not be pleased with me. There are pastors who commit adultery, fornicate, lie, steal, and have jealousy in their hearts and malice on their minds. How can you stand before a congregation with all that riding on your back?

These pastors cannot get anyone delivered because they themselves need deliverance. Do we really care about what the Bible says? This is the reason we cannot cast out demons, heal the sick and diseased, or raise the dead.

"Verily, verily, I say unto you, He that believeth on me, the works that I do shall he do also; and greater works than these shall he do; because I go unto my Father" (John 14:12). Jesus was saying you will do greater works than me because you believe in me, and because you believe I will leave you with power. I am going with my Father, so I will not be with you. I will leave with you the Holy Spirit and the powers that you will need to do my work. Jesus said all these things, yet we don't believe *we* can do them. Can you imagine having the power to raise people from the dead? That's having faith and believing in the power Jesus has given you. Hallelujah!

"For God hath not given us the spirit of fear; but of power, and of love, and of a sound mind" (2 Timothy 1:7). We say we are saved, sanctified, and filled with the Holy Ghost. If that is so, why are we afraid to confront Satan and his imps? Do we not believe Jesus has all power? Do we not believe anything and everything must bow down in Jesus's name? We have the victory already, but we don't believe, so we stay under Satan's control. When we finally submit to God, lie down self-righteousness, and tell Satan to remove his hands from us, we will see a dramatic change in our lives. The lives around us will also be changed.

People in the world look at us and don't want to change their lives. Why would they want to change when churchgoers are doing the same things as people in the world?

"When I say unto the wicked, Thou shalt surely die; and thou givest him not warning, nor speakest to warn the wicked from his wicked way, to save his life; the same wicked man shall die in his iniquity; but his blood will I require at thine hand" (Ezekiel 3:18).

As Jesus's followers, we have the right to speak to the unbeliever. We are trying to save their souls. When we see them saying or doing something wrong, God has given us the power to turn the wicked into good and teach them God's ways. Yet some of us are afraid to speak to the unbeliever because we know we are doing wrong ourselves. Then there are those who are not afraid to speak, even though they know they are doing wrong. These wrongdoers just tell the unbeliever what the Bible says when they themselves do not abide by the Word. How can that be a church of God? Look what we are doing to the people. God created all of us, saved and unsaved alike, so why can't the Christians get it together?

We won't let our members visit another church because we are afraid they are going to like the other churches more and leave ours. If you are a child of God, you cannot hold people in bondage because of your own fears. If God has sent them to your ministry, they will stay, no matter where they may visit. That is telling me that God is not in control of your church. That tells me the church is being run by a person, and whomever is in control will eventually fall. You cannot hold people in bondage because of your insecurities. Your religion becomes a cult when you do this. You are no longer a God-fearing, free-will church.

"Now the Lord is that Spirit: and where the Spirit of the Lord is, there is liberty" (2 Corinthians 3:1). In a Christ-like church, people are able to move and go as they please; this way the Holy Spirit can move freely as well. This is another reason our churches are so weak. We have all sorts of things going on in the pulpit. We all follow protocol, nothing wrong with that. One day I was talking to this pastor and every week he did the same thing, I asked him to allow the Holy Spirit to move try something different this upcoming Sunday, he did just that he allowed the Holy Spirit to move, he said his church haven't been the same. Here are something we allow in God's pulpit. Some say it's ok for these things to go on in a place that suppose to be Holy. Me personally, I think not.

"For there are many unruly and vain talkers and deceivers, especially they of the circumcision" (Titus 1:10).

"If a man also lie with mankind, as he lieth with a woman, both of them have committed an abomination: they shall surely be put to death; their blood shall be upon them" (Leviticus 20:13).

> For this cause God gave them up unto vile affections: for even their women did change the natural use into that which is against nature: and likewise also the men, leaving the natural use of the woman, burned in their lust one toward another; men with men working that which is unseemly, and receiving in themselves that recompense of their error which was met.

> And even as they did not like to retain God in their knowledge, God gave them over to a reprobate mind, to do those things which are not convenient; being filled with all unrighteousness, fornication, wickedness, covetousness, maliciousness; full of envy, murder, debate, deceit, malignity; whisperers, backbiters, haters of God, despiteful, proud, boasters, inventors of evil things, disobedient to parents, without understanding, covenantbreakers, without natural affection, implacable, unmerciful: who knowing the judgment of God, that they which commit such things are

worthy of death, not only do the same, but have pleasure in them that do them. (Romans 1:26–32)

These types of things are going on in our pulpits, but God has given us a way out.

> My little children, these things write I unto you, that ye sin not. And if any man sin, we have an advocate with the Father, Jesus Christ the righteous: and he is the propitiation for our sins: and not for ours only, but also for the sins of the whole world. And hereby we do know that we know him, if we keep his commandments. He that saith, I know him, and keepeth not his commandments, is a liar, and the truth is not in him. But whoso keepeth his word, in him verily is the love of God perfected: hereby know we that we are in him. He that saith he abideth in him ought himself also so to walk, even as he walked. (1 John 2:1–6)

God has given the saved and unsaved people a way out of sin. The Bible tells us to turn from our wicked ways and repent.

"If my people, which are called by my name, shall humble themselves, and pray, and seek my face, and turn from their wicked ways; then will I hear from heaven, and will forgive their sin, and will heal their land" (2 Chronicles 7:14). Who is God talking about here? He's talking about the saved ones He's talking about His people. We have took on so many different customs form around the world that it has cause us to fall into a deep sin and our children and other people can't see God in nothing we do. We have to be an example to our children and this old sinful world. What are we doing that is stopping God from healing our land? Just think about it. Is it really Satan who is stopping our blessings, or is it ourselves? Just think about that. We need to look deep down into our souls and spirits and pray. We need to seek God so He can forgive us of our sins. So this world can be healed. When we are forgiven, we can line our lives up with Christ so we can live eternally. Amen.

The Comeback of God's Pastors

There are a lot of good pastors out here. But the hypocritical pastors make it hard for all pastors. We are lined up with God's Word and doing His will and try to live by God's Word. Of course we all may fall short at times, but we are not out there purposely repeating the same sins over and over. We have a heart after God's own heart and genuinely want to see souls saved.

We are not just talking the talk, we are walking the walk. We are out feeding the hopeless, housing the homeless, healing the sick, casting out demons, and teaching God's Word.

Blessed is the man that walketh not in the counsel of the ungodly, nor standeth in the way of sinners, nor sitteth in the seat of the scornful. But his delight is in the law of the LORD; AND IN HIS LAW DOTH HE MEDITATE DAY AND NIGHT. 3AND HE SHALL BE LIKE A TREE PLANTED BY THE RIVERS OF WATER, THAT BRINGETH FORTH HIS FRUIT IN HIS SEASON: HIS LEAF ALSO SHALL NOT WITHER: AND WHATSOEVER HE DOETH SHALL PROSPER (PSALM 1:1-3)

This psalm is for people who want to do the right thing and grow in the Lord and learn to pray to seek God's guidance. God will prosper those who want him. You do not have to worry about other people moving up; just wait on the Lord and He will exalt you.

We have some great leaders in Christ who seek God's face and want souls to be saved and delivered so we teach the truth of God's Word. We teach the Word that we must live by, and the only way we can do that is by having the Holy Spirit living in us, upon us, and working through us. With God's guidance we cannot go wrong. We must seek, pray, fast, believe, and have faith in the Lord. The true pastors always seek Him first before making a move. I have been in situations where I have listened to people and did not seek God first, and everything I put my hands on failed. But thank God He is a God of second chances! He never removed His grace and mercy from me.

I can remember when God chose me to do his will. I told God, "No, no, no, I can't do this. This is too much for me, Lord. I am shy and can't speak in front of people! Let someone else do it, Lord."

God said, "I chose *you*. I will tell you what to say, when to say it, and how to say it too."

None of that mattered at the time because it was a walk I did not want to take. I was afraid of failing God, something I never wanted to do.

It is in my heart to serve the Lord and God's people, so I got up and did what God told me to do. It has been a blessing to see how God has used me and other pastors to bring people to God. I am not afraid anymore, because God has delivered me from fear.

I remember when I said yes to God. I remember praying and saying, "God, I don't want to bring shame to Your name, so please keep me in all Your ways. I don't want to fail You; You are the one I want to serve. So here I am, Lord. Use me in any way You want."

And that is just what God did and is still doing right now until this day. Not only am I gifted with the Holy Spirit, our family and church are gifted with the Holy Spirit. God really moves when we all get on one accord, seeking God for answers. God shows up every time.

The real pastors come from behind closed doors and step to the forefront. God elevates His small pastors and puts them in places only God can take them. We just need to keep our eyes on Him so we won't get off track. God is raising kings and queens up in the realm of the *true* Holy Spirit, not pretenders. You will know true pastors by the way they speak, live, pray, believe, and their faith in the Word of God. They will not waiver, and when going through a storm will not faint. They won't give up on the Word; they stand strong. Keep the faith in their heart.

Now that we have that done, we need to make sure that when God elevates us, we have already studied the Word of God. We need to study to show ourselves approved. If you want to go to school, go; if not, you can always study for yourself. Get into His Word, know, live, and eat His Word, and let it live in your heart so you will not fail the people God has placed before you.

"Study to shew thyself approved unto God, a workman that needeth not to be ashamed, rightly dividing the word of truth" (2 Timothy 2:15). To study and show yourself approved, get around other true people of God and study the Word, or go to theology school. Get all that you can get and ask God for His wisdom, knowledge, and understanding. You need to understand His Word in order to rightly divide the Word.

Good pastors will be there to support the brokenhearted. We learn to show ourselves approved so we can exalt, uplift, and edify the body of Christ. Yes, some pastors may fall, but we will lift them back up by praying and seeking God for guidance on their behalf. That is what we are supposed to do, care for the lost and bring them to Christ. A good pastor won't leave anyone behind; we help people and carry their loads because sometimes it is too heavy for them to carry alone. We are here for you, and when the load becomes even too heavy for us, we give it to God. The burden carrier.

"Cast thy burden upon the LORD, and he shall sustain thee: he shall never suffer the righteous to be moved" (Psalm 55:22). Even though some pastors have fallen, we are still to treat them with love and respect. We have to treat them just like any person that has fallen. We are here to pray and lift people up and we should do the same for the fallen pastors. So no matter what they have done, we are to lift them up because that's what the Bible tells us to do. Not talk about what is going on in their lives but to bring them back into the body of Christ.

"Saying, Touch not mine anointed, and do my prophets no harm" (Psalm 105:15). This scripture is saying no matter what the pastors have done, we are to keep them in prayer. We are not to go out and tell others what they have done, for that is not of God. If a pastor has harmed you in any way, trust that God will repay you. We all know that some pastors call on the name of the Lord but are not walking it; they are merely talking and having a form of godliness. Still we can't touch them, pray for them.

"Dearly beloved, avenge not yourselves, but rather give place unto wrath: for it is written, Vengeance is mine; I will repay, saith the Lord" (Romans 12:19). So it does not matter what was done or said to you by anyone. God will repay you for all the hurt and sorrow people have put you through, even if it was a pastor. God will avenge you.

We as pastors should not let our good be evil spoken of (see Romans 14:16). Sometimes when we do good things, people perceive them as wrong. That is why we should try not to judge or talk about what someone is doing. You don't know what God told that pastor to do or say because the Lord did not speak to *you* about it.

"Then went the Pharisees, and took counsel how they might entangle him in his talk. And they sent out unto him their disciples with the Herodians, saying, Master, we know that thou art true, and teachest the way of God in truth, neither carest thou for any man: for thou regardest not the person of men" (Matthew 22:15–16). Look how they tried to speak evil against Jesus. Think of what more they will do to us; Jesus was perfect in all His ways. There are always people looking for something wrong in you, especially if you are trying to live for God. So I tell you today, try to stay away from evil, because as pastors, we are always on the frontline. Be true to yourself and practice what you preach. Someone is always watching and waiting for you to slip up.

Despite all the good Jesus did, people still wanted to make Him seem evil. No matter what you do, someone is always going to be out to defame your character. We need to stand together in times like these, but we won't because even some of the pastors pull each other down. What a shame, because we are leaders of God's Word. How can we lead when we are steadily beating up on each other? There are enough people in the world for your congregation and mine, so let's stop, and pull together. We are all fighting for the same things: to win souls over for God's kingdom. The people need a leader; they need guidance from godly men and women. How can they be led without a preacher?

"How then shall they call on him in whom they have not believed? and how shall they believe in him of whom they have not heard? and how shall they hear without a preacher?" (Romans 10:14).

"Let your speech be always with grace, seasoned with salt, that ye may know how ye ought to answer every man" (Colossians 4:6). As pastors, we have to analyze what we say. It should always line up with the Word of God. The words that come from a pastor's mouth should come forth to heal, correct, exalt, and enlighten the body of Christ. Every word and action should be thought through and prayed about before we speak and do. Our words should always be graceful.

I am not saying you have to say a long, drawn-out prayer all the time. You can say a prayer to yourself asking God to speak through you. We must humble ourselves before we enter the pulpit. We may all have good intentions, but sometimes life situations or emotions get in the way.

"Seek the LORD and his strength, seek his face continually" (1 Chronicles 16:11). If we seek the Lord's face, it tells us He will show up. He will give us a sign and send someone with confirmation. He is not feeble when it comes to His people. God will always answer the true and upright. I have never seen the righteous forsaken; God is always right on time.

"And we have known and believed the love that God hath to us. God is love; and he that dwelleth in love dwelleth in God, and God in him" (1 John 4:16). The good pastors who have God dwelling in them show many signs of love, caring, humility; meekness, gentleness, and faithfulness, for all those are characteristics of God. You will know a true pastor by the way he or she loves and treats other people. God loves and has given His only son Jesus Christ. Can you really say you love like God? His love is unconditional and does not expect anything in return. His love is genuine, free, giving, honest, and spiritual, the agape love.

> 4 Charity suffereth long: and is kind: charity envieth not: charity vaunteth not itself: is not puffedup: 5 doth not behave itself unseemly: seeketh not her own: is not easily provoked. Thinketh no evil. 6rejoiceth not in iniquity: but rejoiceth in the truth: 7 beareth all things, believeth all things, hopeth all things, endureth all things (1 Corinthians 13:4-7)

If we always stay on the same course, love will never fail. It will set out for what it is meant to do as long as you have faith in Jesus. As pastors, we sometimes beat ourselves up when we fall. However, we need to realize that we are only human and are not going to hit the mark all the time. We see things we want and need, but it is not always the time for us to receive those things. Even knowing that, we step out on faith looking for God to give us the answer we are looking for, but *our* answer is not *His* answer. A lot of the time we find that out through trial and error. If we had only waited a little while longer, *His* answer would have showed up.

It rains on the just, just as it rains on the unjust. We have to know how to stand in the face of a storm. When it comes to God answering our prayers, we need to believe and have faith, hope, and love. I know from experience that we can pray for people, but when we pray for ourselves, it seems as if God doesn't hear us. We often wonder if He is listening. I have prayed many times for others, and I would see their blessings manifest right away. On the other hand, it seems as if my blessings will never come to pass. No matter what you think of the situation, you must hold fast to your prayer; you will be answered. Keep the faith and do not move too hastily. God knows what you need and when you need it. Withstand the test.

Stay strong in the Word of God so you can receive your rewards on Earth, because we have no use for them in heaven. I don't know about you, but I want my blessings and miracles right here on Earth while I live. Stop beating yourself up; you did not fall on purpose. Even in the natural when someone trips and falls, it is an accident. You must pick yourself up (it will be a little humiliating sometimes) and continue on your way. Just because you fall sometimes does not put you in the category with the pastors who are doing and saying anything they want without any instruction from the Lord. The blood *will* be on their hands come judgment. *You* must get up because this is *your* comeback.

Life is wonderful as a pastor. Have you ever taken the time to look through a pastor's eyes? Do you see what they see? Do you feel what they feel? Do you go where they go? For all the naysayers, can you walk in a pastor's shoes? Can you stay up all night and intercede for someone to get a breakthrough? Are you willing to get up at three in the morning when you get a call from one of you partners asking you to meet them at the hospital because there has been an accident? Are you willing to pick multiple people up for church or fix a meal for the entire congregation? Are you willing to give the congregation an appreciation day? Pastors have a hard enough job to do without someone trying to put down God's chosen ones.

Will your response be, "No, I am the pastor, and I don't do those things"? There are some awesome pastors out there who are willing to help. All you need to do is give them your hand and follow them as they follow Christ.

"To every thing there is a season, and a time to every purpose under the heaven" (Ecclesiastes 3:1). Sometimes, people go through a storm and have not done anything wrong; it's just a season of pitfall. Just keep looking up. God has got you.

I remember this bishop would always say, "If you fall, keep moving in the Lord." That man of God taught me a great deal about the Word of God, and people. He was excellent in God's Word. He taught *and* lived the Word and inspired me to go further.

"Whoso despiseth the word shall be destroyed: but he that feareth the commandment shall be rewarded" (Proverbs 13:13). Do not be dismayed in following the commandments.

"And let us not be weary in well doing: for in due season we shall reap, if we faint not" (Galatians 6:9). Pastors have a blessing in Christ as long as we keep the faith. Many pastors have stopped preaching the Word of God because they have burned out. I am here to tell you not to throw in the towel. God sees all the lonely nights you stay up praying and seeking His face. Fret not; your blessing is here now. You have stood the test of time, and God is speaking to you. Your comeback will blow the world's mind! They wanted you to fall but you stood.

The good pastors get kicked to the curb because they are not with the in crowd. Thank God people do not elevate you. It is a blessing that God does the elevating. Your elevation is coming! You have shown yourself approved and have stood on God's Word. When everyone threw darts at you, you did not sway.

If a church walked away from you without a cause, God will give you back plenty for your faithfulness. The family that walked away from you because they did not see anything changing in your life, God is saying to the naysayers, "Look at them now!" God's Word will never fail.

"For with God nothing shall be impossible" (Luke 1:37). Sometimes being a pastor is a lonely road. Your father, mother, children, siblings, aunts, uncles, cousins, and friends may help you sometimes, but we as pastors have to sit alone and wonder what God is up to. He may not always answer you right away, but remember this: when there is no answer, God wants you to stand still and let Him work.

Yes, we may live a lonely life, but it is all worth it in the end. Sometimes you may want to go out and enjoy yourself, but on the other hand, when you think about what you have to lose, you'll say it is not worth it: I love who I am, what I do, and I love living the life of Christ. Being a true pastor means you may have to stand even if you have to stand alone. The good pastors are the comeback for the bad pastors.

"Bless them which persecute you: bless, and curse not" (Romans 12:14). We go through a lot of chaos because we want to do what was put in our hearts by God. There is always someone trying to throw salt in the game. People try to make you stagnant so you may stop whatever God is trying to do through you. You know the God we serve. You cannot stop what God has started;

you may slow it down, but you will never stop it. When God has put something inside you, it will get done. If God did not want it to happen, He would not have put it in you. Wake up and walk into your calling. Always seek God's guidance.

We strive to win souls. We did not become pastors to strive for money. As pastors with discernment, we can see what is inside you. We know that God can bring you out of shyness, low self-esteem, drugs, homosexuality, lying, murderous thoughts, jealousy, envy, fornication, and adultery. A pastor who is truly filled with the spirit of God can see these things in a person. These people are in bondage, and some of these pastors are in bondage also. The pastors will never admit that they are in bondage.

Whether you are a good or bad pastor, we all need prayer. The walk of a pastor is not an easy walk. Would you like to walk in a pastor's shoes? With all the problems the world brings to the pastors, they still must deal with their own lives. With God and His anointing on our lives, we complete all tasks put before us.

"Bless them which persecute you: bless, and curse not" (Romans 12:14). When people do you wrong, the Bible tells us to bless them and not curse them. Don't you know we have the power to curse in our hands? God does not want that; He would rather we humble ourselves and seek Him. I cannot do anything to you that God cannot do better. To all friends and so-called pastors, I do not want to hurt or harm you in any way. I just want to love with the agape love of Jesus Christ.

"Let every soul be subject unto the higher powers. For there is no power but of God: the powers that be are ordained of God" (Romans 13:1). Everyone must submit to God's authority, for all authority comes from God. How can we say we are God's children when we cannot even submit to His authority? We say we are followers of Christ, but are we really? The true Christians will take a stand, even if it means taking a backseat and letting the wrong person be glorified for a while. When we submit to God, He stands up for us. No battle is too big or too small; God fights them all and always wins. There is no power that can withstand the blow of God. God is our avenger, and our battle is already won. Now all we have to do is save some souls for God's kingdom. There is no power but of God.

"Let no corrupt communication proceed out of your mouth, but that which is good to the use of edifying, that it may minister grace unto the hearers" (Ephesians 4:29). This is what the good pastors should stand on, nothing but the Word of God. Good things will come from a true pastor. When the people hear it, it shall be like fire coming from their mouths that shall heal the land. God wants us to speak as Jesus did when he walked the earth. Talk to the congregation, and we shall allow God to move and do a work in someone's life.

"I can do all things through Christ which strengtheneth me" (Philippians 4:13). As pastors, we cannot do anything outside of God. God is the one who orchestrates our comings and goings. He gives us the strength and power through the Holy Spirit to see people's pain or see them headed for destruction. God has anointed his true pastors to heal the people. We cannot do anything without the Lord; it would be like chancing the wind; we wouldn't know which way to go. Thank God for His Holy Spirit that lives inside the Christians.

"And I will pray the Father, and he shall give you another Comforter, that he may abide with you for ever; even the Spirit of truth; whom the world cannot receive, because it seeth him not, neither knoweth him: but ye know him; for he dwelleth with you, and shall be in you" (John 14:16–17). Jesus is talking to His disciples and basically says, "I will give you another advocate to help you and be with you forever." This is the spirit of truth; you know Him, for he lives with you and will be in you. Jesus promised that when He left, His spirit would live inside the Christian people. That is from which we draw all power. We cannot even try to prophesy without His strength and power living in us. A true pastor knows we cannot do it alone, so we stand before God and wait on His answer before we move. The waiting may be long, but there is a blessing at the end. That is what makes the difference. Just to see people's lives change means a lot to the true Word-speaking pastors.

The faithful, honest, and true believing pastors are shunned and put down by our counterparts. They want people to believe we are too inferior to preach the Word of God. But when they show up and see the anointing of God upon us, they are surprised by the power of God that is working through us. When we are quiet and not out in front boasting or seeking what we can take from someone, we are put down.

We don't boast about ourselves. The people God puts before you will edify and exalt you through the Word of God. I have never seen so many false and phony Christians in my entire fifteen years of preaching. We covet what other pastors have, not knowing God has blessed each pastor with what God wants them to have. So stop hating on each other; we are all in this Christian walk together, for one purpose: to save souls for the kingdom of God. So you faithful, anointed, believing pastors, keep doing the will of God, no matter who puts you down. Keep being you, because there is a blessing in the end.

I remember one time I was supposed to speak at a church event. Other pastors talked among themselves and dissuaded the church from letting me preach. What kind of thing is that to do in the body of Christ? Aren't we all supposed to be in this thing for Christ Jesus? The true pastors deal with jealousy simply because they are anointed. I did not give myself this anointing, just as you did not give yourself the anointing. God gave each person what He wanted them to have.

We wonder why people come into church and leave the same way they came in. It is because the pastors are so busy being envious of one another that we have no power to get God's people delivered. It will take a strong pastor to stand up to the demonic spirits that some pastors let operate around and with them. The pastors know it is not right but still allow it because of prestige, power, and wealth. They may look like they've got it all together, but on the inside, they do not know what to do.

This is what makes true pastors look bad even when they are trying to live right in the sight of God. There really are some good pastors out there who truly care for people's souls well-being. We have taken a step back, but it is time to stand up now! If we do not, the bad pastors will take a lot of souls to hell with them.

All true pastors, come to the forefront. Stand up and be noticed, for now is your season to be blessed. You have been sitting for too long! Let's take back God's kingdom! Amen.

O Lord, thou knowest: remember me, and visit me, and revenge me of my persecutors; take me not away in thy longsuffering: know that for thy sake I have suffered rebuke. Thy words were found, and I did eat them; and thy word was unto me the joy and rejoicing of mine heart: for I am called by thy name, O Lord, God of hosts.

I sat not in the assembly of the mockers, nor rejoiced; I sat alone because of thy hand: for thou hast filled me with indignation. Why is my pain perpetual, and my wound incurable, which refuseth to be healed? wilt thou be altogether unto me as a liar, and as waters that fail?

Therefore thus saith the Lord, If thou return, then will I bring thee again, and thou shalt stand before me: and if thou take forth the precious from the vile, thou shalt be as my mouth: let them return unto thee; but return not thou unto them. And I will make thee unto this people a fenced brasen wall: and they shall fight against thee, but they shall not prevail against thee: for I am with thee to save thee and to deliver thee, saith the Lord. And I will deliver thee out of the hand of the wicked, and I will redeem thee out of the hand of the terrible. (Jeremiah 15:15–21)

God will protect His people, the ones who do right. The ones who do wrong will be dealt with accordingly, so take notice of your actions. "Now faith is the substance of things hoped for, the evidence of things not seen. For by it the elders obtained a good report. Through faith we understand that the worlds were framed by the word of God, so that things which are seen were not made of things which do appear" (Hebrews 11:1–3).

Do you have faith in things you don't see? Or is it only in what you see? Your faith need to be strong in things you don't see and know that it will come to pass by the power of God .We are going to talk here about the leaders of a congregation. Your faith depends of the faith of the leader. So leaders, what kind of faith do you have? Is it only be leaving in what you see, then that's not faith. Is it wavering faith that determines your congregations' faith? If you have little faith, then your congregation will have little faith. If you have big faith, your congregation will fall in line. Do you have faith that is hot one day and cold the next? I wonder.

"But let him ask in faith, nothing wavering. For he that wavereth is like a wave of the sea driven with the wind and tossed" (James 1:6). Take a look at yourself, and then take a look at your congregation. Can you say your faith is in the right place? Is it wavering faith or true faith that will see, obey, honor, protect, love, and offer peace? We often talk about the congregation, but what if we looked at the ones leading the congregation? What is their life like? A person does not have to live at home with you to know how your life is away from the church. A spirit identifies with kindred spirits, whether good or evil.

"Beloved, believe not every spirit, but try the spirits whether they are of God: because many false prophets are gone out into the world" (1 John 4:1). These false prophets may be in the pulpit or the congregation. Wherever they are, you will know them by the fruit they produce. Good will produce good, just as bad will produce bad. I know the pastors who have been behind the scenes are now coming to the forefront. God is elevating them now in times like these. He is elevating the ones who didn't mind waiting on the Lord. If you are seeking a true pastor, you will find one; just continue to look. We are out there.

"If any man will do his will, he shall know of the doctrine, whether it be of God, or whether I speak of myself" (John 7:17). Experienced pastors will know to keep the Word of God and nothing but God's Word flowing out of their mouths. They must be anointed and appointed by God to stay relevant.

At our last women's conference, the leaders we chose to speak were right on point with what we needed at the time. Our church was going through a storm, but God made a way. The words the speakers spoke were so applicable to our situation that it was as if God Himself were in the room. No one in attendance left the church that evening the same way they came in. If you entered the doors spiritually dead, you left full of life. You could just see and feel the atmosphere change. There was real power in the church that evening.

"It is the spirit that quickeneth; the flesh profiteth nothing: the words that I speak unto you, they are spirit, and they are life" (John 6:63). God's spirit alone gives life. We can do nothing unless His Holy Spirit lives in us. The words we speak mean nothing if we do not have His spirit living and working in us. So pastors and Christians let us be a good example to the world. When they see us they should see the one who lives on the inside not the flesh. We have some very large shoes to fill so let's fill it with power and love.

"Being born again, not of corruptible seed, but of incorruptible, by the word of God, which liveth and abideth for ever" (1 Peter 1:23). To the Christians and non-Christians, we have leaders out in front who seek God for sermons and answers before speaking. We are born again of incorruptible seed, God's seed, which lives and abides in us forever. We seek out to do what is in God's Word, not looking at our needs but looking after the needs of others, to serve, exalt, and lift up the people in the name of Jesus. We are to bring the hurting and the lost to Christ to show them that there is a better way. We are there to hold their hands until they can stand on their own.

As pastors, we are in a leadership position. We must do better, because Satan is on his job all day, every day. We must be on our job even more. If we say we are called and chosen, then we need to be about His work, not just talking about it. Anyone can talk the talk, but can you live it? God's people, let's get it together to win the people for God's kingdom. Amen.

Printed in the United States
by Baker & Taylor Publisher Services